DATE DUE			
~~Oct 7'74~~			

GETTING DRUNK
WITH THE
BIRDS

OHIO UNIVERSITY PRESS
ATHENS

GETTING DRUNK WITH THE BIRDS

by Richard Frost

Library of Congress Catalog Number LC72-141383
ISBN 8214-0088-6
Manufactured in the United States of America by
Oberlin Printing Company
Design by Irving Perkins

ACKNOWLEDGMENTS

Acknowledgement is made to the following periodicals, in which most of the poems in this volume originally appeared:

The Beloit Poetry Journal
Carleton Miscellany
The English Journal
The New Orleans Review
Poetry Northwest
Prairie Schooner
Southwest Review
TriQuarterly

FOR CAROL

Contents

GETTING DRUNK
WITH THE
BIRDS

Jean Ingres' *Le Bain Turc*

At eighty-three he painted this: twenty-four naked women
who clearly wouldn't care if they found themselves watched.
(The frame is round, like the field in a telescope.)
Over on the right, wearing a ruby necklace,
is a sleepy redhead with her forearms behind her neck
in that timeless pose, and she partly obscures
two others so that you can't tell whether one of them
is fondling her own breast or the other is doing it.
Except that when you look at their faces, you know which one.
It is all very mysterious, very Eastern.
On the left, one girl is dangling her long legs
in the pool, and right behind her on tiptoe,
waving her arms, another is dancing delicately
to a tambourine played by a big Negress.
Off in the background there are more women, gossiping
or just lolling around. Some of them are eating things,
their heads thrown back in abandon. You feel sure
that Ingres knew exactly what he was doing.
There is a table in the immediate foreground
holding a few sweetmeats and cups, and a vase is floating
in mid-air right in front of the table, attracting
absolutely no attention in this environment.
Ingres must have posed twenty-four live models
and set to work busily. You feel sure of this
until you notice that the woman with the mandolin
is exactly as he painted her fifty-five years before
by herself sitting on a bed. She was not
there, looking that well, fifty-five years later
when in the fine Turkish climate of his imagination
Ingres placed those ladies where they are waiting.
The water laps in the pool, the mandolin
and castanets pluck at our senses,
and a brown-eyed slave squeezes an atomizer
of perfume into the long blonde hair
of one favorite, while Ingres folds up his paints,
rubs his chin, smiles, and lives three years more.

To Aunt Jo, Leaving Me

Dear Aunt, it is September now by this sea
where I came to write anyway. You said
what you knew about the meaning of money.
But some of this would please you. I have put up
on a terrace below the house a bamboo fence
before an area to be used as a garbage dump.
Gradually the garbage is filling in—a layer
of bottles, egg shells, cereal boxes, coffee grounds, bones,
covered with a little dirt to confuse the flies,
then more garbage. The ants have found this storehouse,
developing colonies upon its promise.
For days now I've watched their lines of supply
grow wider and more complicated, across
a branch and down the trunk, onto the pile
and back onto the hillside where they can't be followed.
I know you would have admired their common sense.

Then there is a neat young lizard
who shows up every evening near a light bulb,
his white throat and belly and tail on the other side
of the sunporch glass, catching moths and flies
with our electricity. The first lizard
left the night I tried to catch him. Carefully swinging
the window inside, with the lizard still on the glass,
I took hold of his tail, and the lizard simply left.
There was no tug, and very little blood,
and I was holding a live tail, which twisted
for several minutes on the tile floor
until I threw it out—a breakaway tail.
Perhaps the lizard ran over and put it back on.
I try to find lessons you would have seen.

At night I sleep under a mosquito net,
and when I kill one of those whining feeders
with a rolled manuscript while he rests on the ceiling,
there's a bright smear of my blood. Everyone
should do with what he has.

But it's all so lovely

here, that I find it hard to be practical.
The ocean glistens below my balcony
as if its salt were proudly reflecting the light
from every facet. The terraces of grapes,
mimosa, lemons, almonds, morning glories
descend to the sand, and a green and white sail
moves in the harbor. Overhead the sun
takes its own sweet time, and the blue sky
this coast is named for, the sky holds perfectly
over the whole land, to Italy, to Spain
and out over the sea. And everything
in the sandy soil grows pleasantly
with the rich nitrates and sunshine and water
and plenty of good worms.

Yet I am reminded,

warmed by all this beautiful give and take,
of you and the things you always explained about saving.
For you have died, dear probably virgin Jo,
leaving seventy-five thousand dollars
to a half sister none of us can remember.
Your body was sent to Michigan, your clothes
were given to charity, your house was sold.
Here in the clear light, I would like you to know
I am up to nothing but good. The sea is dancing
and I am writing verses. The terraces glow
with life. The mosquitoes and ants, everything
will be eating enough. Below the house, where I fenced it,
my sanitary landfill grows and grows.

Locking Out

Working diligently all afternoon,
I have repaired the lock in the back door.
Driving home from a morning class,
I passed along a shining corridor
Of October leaves, and because we turn so soon,
because of the color falling like lives, *Alas,*
    I thought, and cried.

Our house crouches on its high terrace.
We climb a narrow path. Below, the sea
hollers at our bricks. We have a lock
for solid reasons. Past the garden is a tree
that was old a hundred years before us.
One day an owner planted it and walked
    toward the house

out of the scarlet wood, but the leaves collared him close,
and where the path widened he stumbled, and night entered
  forcibly.

The Banquet

After the observations by J. H. Fabre

Dung beetle, grave and sacred scarab, you shape
the enormous savory ball and, using your forehead
and bandy legs, butt it toward somewhere
to dig a parlor. It almost always happens
that you have hardly begun forcing the toothsome
prize across a field or down a road,
when another beetle wants to share the burden.
You know he is not doing this because he likes you,
and you don't need help. Yet all you do
in protest is to keep the key position,
pushing. You let him pull, stupidly
in front, demonstrating his uselessness.
It is not easy to be the real owner.
You roll and fall, shove, kick dust, until
you reach a place, and you set about digging
the deep refectory. The other beetle
pretends to go to sleep on top of the orb.
Then when you have tunneled out of sight,
your guest climbs down and tries to steal your treasure.
But you have been watching, and you leap out of the hole.
The thief now pretends to be supporting the bolus
on a hillside, frantically propping himself against it.
You approach him and gesture with your mandibles.
Then you both move the ball back to the burrow,
which by this time seems spacious enough.

In goes the globe, the entrance to the corridor
is closed, and deep in reconciling shade,
in the friendly warm dampness, you sit down
and solemnly commence the banquet which lasts
for two months. Never even pausing
for a second, day or night, you eat
and eat the sphere, constant as a pair of clocks.
Finally, neither of you could say whether
it was better or worse that you met. Here was pleasure.
Really, there had been little quarreling,
and one's paunch is hideously like that of another.

never falling.
leaning but
thin ladder,
and climb a
filling our heads
their warm song
we must imagine
Nearing the bells,
to each gallery.
turns us darkly
inside this tower
changing angles
The long spiral
curves to the sea.
the bright Arno
rooftops shrink,
drop farther away,
Now the avenues
have climbed in.
thousands like us
worn by leather
on marble steps
finding a balance
of our promises,
how to keep all
here we may see
Love,

Climbing the Tower at Pisa

Getting Drunk With the Birds

Like ravenous ornaments eating their own tree,
the robins tear at the pyrecantha bush,
swallowing berries until, obscenely drunk,
they walk all over the driveway, shitting and trying
to fly, sailing up sideways and almost backwards
to the wires, only to tumble down and walk some more,
wings adrag and tails fallen.
This treacherous botany lays them out for the cats,
who are at first suspicious, never having seen
so many birds so easy to spring at, birds
who hardly care to peep for their necks—too many to eat,
scattering clumsily, feathers and crunching bird bones.
Yet they must all be killed, and the garden
is full of shivering cats, flattened and charging
until we sweep into the yard with our sobering brooms.

In South Africa drunken elephants
become a problem every winter, eating
fermented berries from the maroela trees
and stumbling into villages, all over
automobiles, mailboxes, people, rose trellises,
and finally have to be shot. Your city
is probably full of drunk animals killing
and getting killed and having parties, the cats
sneaking soberly behind the hedge
until the right second for crashing in, the lights
going out, the elephants arriving late
from another party, setting the house on fire,
the wheel starting to spin, the center falling.

Only a few of us get away in our cars
to the cool freeways, the world flaming a mile
to left and right of our corridor, and we drive
the quiet night until, ahead, toward us,
charging and screeching, horns and high beams
burning farther than ears or eyes can tell,
come the big sedans full of drunk families
going home, their mufflers dragging sparks
along the pavement, windows and doors open,
bottles flying toward poles and signboards, radios
all on the same station. We pull onto the shoulder
and watch everyone go by: the Liberals
and Klansmen, the sleepins, the Union leaders, the National
Guardsmen, the high school Principals, the Democrats,
Hell's Angels, the Pope, the Welcome Wagons,
the Summerlane children, the F.B.I., the Editors,
the Britannica salesmen, the Republicans, the girls
from Smith College, the Bomb Planners and Banners,
the Bombers, the Pop painters, the Objectivist poets,
the Justice impeachers. It gives us time to think
about those relatives we shouldn't leave,
about our jobs and houses, time to turn
around, after the same white line, straight
as determined drunks can drive to their own city
at the end of a terrible day. Then we are passing
the used car lots and Mabel's Drive Inn—
it looks so familiar, as if we had never left;
and the way we feel, it doesn't matter what we
or the birds have done. It's fun to be having it,
this great shoving weekend we have earned. Give everyone
a drink, starting right now. And get out of our way.

A Painting by Breughel

In shorts and what is called a halter, she pedals,
rings a bell, transistor portable
playing from handlebar. On evening porches
husbands watch and smile as her dark hair swings.

Couples stroll, stars burst for the Fourth of July,
boys scare girls with illegal cherry bombs.
A band's hard voltage rocks from the Courthouse lawn
into street dancers who earnestly gesture and cling.

Why is she riding the bike and ringing the bell?
Where are couples strolling? Why scare girls?
What is the point of dancing in the street?
What sort of answer should these questions bring?

A painting by Breughel showed, when cleaned, beneath
what had seemed to be only a country dance,
a village orgy, with everyone's privates unmasked.
Someone had retouched the embarrassing thing.

Notes On Survival

Reading accounts of castaways, one is astounded
at the high incidence of cannibalism.
Aside from the famous example of the Donner party
and those terrible stories of the railroad cars
full of Jews or Russian prisoners, arriving
at concentration camps after miles in freezing weather
with some of the dead eaten by the few left alive
(proof of their bestiality, the SS said)—
aside from these examples, there are hundreds of records
of humans eating humans to survive
and feeling amazed at the time that they could do it.
The liver, the brain and the blood seem to have been
actually relished at times. In 1826
Miss Ann Saunders, becalmed on the ship
of Captain John Kendall, ate her fiancee,
John Fryer, declaring in her hunger
it was the most delicious thing she had ever tasted.
So finally we must face the possibility
that if the liner we are vacationing on
gets lost, or the jet plane coasts onto an island,
radios broken, off the charts and running
out of turtle soup and Chateaubriand,
all the Scotch gone, and no comfort in the movies,
nothing in sight but coral and plankton, nothing—
any of us could get the idea before it was mentioned,
perhaps being the first to suggest drawing straws.
There is serious consolation when one reads
the journal of Robert Scott, the Antarctic explorer
who died with his men eleven miles from a depot.

Dying of cold and starvation, nothing but whirling
drifts outside the tent, Scott kept his diary
in vivid and beautiful style right to the end.
After several of the men were dead, the rest went on
for the last few days on tea and a few crumbs of pemmican.
Who in his sober mind can tell how noble
or how mistaken the restraint? In any case,
it is not that man is a beast that is most surprising,
but that when everything requires it, he sometimes isn't.
At last Scott had written, "the end cannot be far.
It seems a pity, but I do not think I can write more.
For God's sake, look after our people."

Test On the *Odyssey*

Odysseus sailed until he was Ulysses
and Aphrodite, Venus. Name the names.
After the fight in the hall, what must be done?
What metaphor is there in Circe's potion?

Do you feel that it is Homer's intention
to hold his men responsible?
Does Zeus pull strings to run them through their rimes?
Define "Homeric hero" accurately.

How does Odysseus change, or doesn't he?
Describe Greek attitudes on guests and games.
What was death, and was there any Hell?
Explain how war sometimes affects a nation
when the leader leaves.
                                        Clear illustrations
must be given. Write the answers plainly.
Fold your papers at the final bell.
The best marks will be gifts of bright Athene.

Moving Out

The overpass predicted across our house,
the beercans imminent, we buy a farm.
Stumbling around the barn, I wonder where
the highway is following me. Hammered onto the bark
of my pines and my oaks, my No Trespassing signs hold firm,
and I tread confidently into my pasture.
My woodchucks waddle, my fat rabbits circle,
trout wait in my pond. My sky spreads rosily
over the herd of deer in archery season.
The trouble is, I am the same poet.
I must buy gravel to cover the rusting cans
of the last owner's dump. There is a dead frog
in the spring. I never was handed a form
I could manage, and sooner or later these acres
will be shabbier than the cow I hopefully bought.
The horses won't rhyme with the clover, the chickens won't scan,
the route between the toilet and septic tank
will somehow confuse the critics. Then, comfortable
with the whole muddy place, I will turn out yards
and truckloads of some unrecognizeable vegetable
that will enjoy brief popularity stewed at the drunk mission
and then be pickled for first year botany classes.
Finally the highway or a cemetery or a library
will begin to construct itself before my eyes,
and I will probably move back to the city,
carrying with me the only soil I have owned.

What It Might Be Like If A Certain Type of Romantic Poet Became President With Or Without His Knowing It

How interesting, those marks on his wall
where the chimney gagged with soot:
two dancers trembled and kissed until
they blended, breast and foot.

And while he watched the metaphor
spread down the plaster,
a black man sang at his side door
some stuff about disaster.

The helpless dancers bulged and turned
into a fat buffoon.
In the back lot, Asia burned
a delicate napalm brown.

The swelling jester merged with the roof
and rug, becoming a column
of tar, live poetic proof
of a theme profound and solemn,

he knew. But what? He'd always been graceful
and clever in phrasing it. Smoke
began to thread in. One good face full
and puff! his talents awoke.

"It's me! It's I. Why didn't I guess it
at once? Those marks are my soul
blending with everything. Now to express it."
He jumped to his desk, but a hole

had raced him there, and before he could sit
he dropped into the inferno.
Body and spirit sizzled and spat
and fumed until there were no

marks of the poet. Nothing rose
out of the ashes filling
his empty land, where his unchosen
subjects were angrily milling.

The Poet's Wife

"Look at the parole wagons,"
you say. I love you.
"*Patrol* wagons."
"O.K. Don't get your dandruff up."
"Your mind, it's amazing."
"Really? Are we going to a movie?"
"Ah, what about the dishes?"
"I did them. Didn't you hear me?
Well, I was in there
washing them like a hawk."

From the House Top

And after all, will you be froward, will you be peevish, will you be sullen, will you be ill-natured, will you be unfaithful or neglectful? No! Heaven forbid it! It is better to dwell alone on the housetop, than to dwell with a brawling woman in a wide house.

MEMOIRS OF THE REV. AMMIE ROGERS, A.M.

Reverend Rogers, from here on my shingles
  I can see you clinging to yours.
The stars are a sermon, the clean air tingles,
  yet I think I'll go back indoors.

Reverend Rogers, I don't want to quit.
  You've led me with precept and prayer.
But I can't find anyplace to sit,
  and I'd like to be down in my chair.

Reverend Rogers, my wife is froward,
  peevish, sullen, brawling,
unfaithful, neglectful, ill-natured,
  and . . . Give me your hand, I'm falling!

After Rains

After the first rains it is again clear.
Mosquitoes are back inside this humid bedroom,
whining and raising welts on elbows. Yesterday
a cripple with an alto saxophone,
a can of coins and a sign describing his illness
performed in the market. The poor bleating made me wonder
whether he'd played too long or just begun.

Or perhaps he needed a new reed. I drove home,
straddling ditches the rain has worn in our road.
Now it's almost dawn. Mosquitoes whine
and push their needles through the net for blood,
begging insanely. Somewhere between their song
and the moan of a wrecked musician, I dig my pen
into paper grown limp in the saturated air.

And at my back in this bed in a borrowed house,
you sleep as you have through thousands of lines, lovely
and comfortable, grown so used by now
to my routines that I seem not to disturb you.
In a world of mad needling and sad need,
I could but turn, and my words would stop climbing thinly.
Yet I work. You sleep like the rain, like another poem.

When the Buzzards Come Back
To Hinckley, Ohio

Love, where I have learned about inconstancy
from you, these birds for over a hundred and fifty
years with the flap and scramble and bad breath
have been clever enough to return on the same day,
for which they are honored. Perhaps if you could order
your migrations so they fell in some interesting pattern
against the calendar, we could sell a biography
or even a t.v. spectacular, my slattern,
my morsel, my black eyes, my sweet-beaked lady buzzard.

For Fran

Roughly forty per-cent of my time this month
will be spent writing a poem. Every rhyme
and every last loose foot I will think
and think about from when the late news
goes off, until the man comes on at six-thirty
to talk about Aristophanes. Reason
and feeling, thought and intuition, I
will put onto these pieces of blank
paper, and I will write this new poem.

During the day I will sleep, and you and our children
will run the house. In my head I will always hear you
closing doors and setting the table. Then
one morning, I will hand you the folded page,
and you will all read it at breakfast. After
that I will sleep little for several days,
dreaming of something to do.
                                        This way we'll go on
for years, probably, during our Easter
holidays and summer vacations and all
through my sabbaticals and even while
one of us is terribly sick. Eventually
you or I will die, and then the other,
and we will have been alive in the ways we could be.
My watching it happen, that is our separation.

When My Camera Went Bad

"Monsieur, it was the camera," he said, taking a pin
and scratching little pictures in the black emulsion,
pictures of ships, fish, houses, people,
until he had made about ten new slides
out of the useless ones.
"Anyway," he said, "you can take the bad slides
and make the pictures you lost.
Here is Paris. Here is Salzburg."

Letter To A Landlord

Whittaker, the mice are knocking things
around your attic, under the tiles, behind
a door I cannot find. They gallop at night.
Sometimes I hear them sawing and chiseling.

Is the door to the mice inside the locked cupboard?
Whittaker, they are stealing our almonds,
neatly biting off the ends. They are making nests
in the eaves. Often I have surprised them.

On the sunporch they have been surveying the refrigerator
with their pointed faces and naked tails.
What they intend I don't know.
There are many, many of them in the walls.

You may point to the many obvious rats in this world,
out in the open, gnawing at our foundations,
but I think of those small cute mice getting rich in their tunnel—
selling bombs to the rats, probably. They are my kind of problem.

The Blue Coast

The old Russian caretaker stops me, his eyes
furious. "DeGaulle is a Jew, really. I
have discovered this. He is no Catholic."
The avenues are glutted cheek-to-cheek,
shoving and hating. It is noon in Europe.
The young Italian explains, "If there were no Jews,
we would have peace. Really, Mussolini
was very brilliant, but we no longer can buy
his books. The Jews are behind everything.
They killed Kennedy and put in Johnson.
They are causing the trouble in Asia. Kennedy,
for me, he was the best. The Jews are rotten."
We are lying on the beach. Motorboats
and sails, the perfect sky. The *Michaelangelo*
rests in the harbor, the lighters carry
passengers from her and to her. Carefully I get up
and leave for the house I borrowed, up in a grove
of mimosa trees. The two German shepherds
bark and run at their gate as I walk past them
and up the dirt road. Below, cars race
on the coast highway, and an express train shudders by . . .
"I was at Auschwitz," says the Belgian lady.
"When the Russians came, they had to stop the Polish
political prisoners from trampling the Jews to death.
They hated us so. But what could you expect
from those filthy Poles?" There is a fine dust
on the trees and fences. From here the valley runs
to the half-moon of the shore, and the sand is hidden
behind the new hotels. Cezanne once roamed
these hills, or ones not far from here, like these,

with his brown canvas carrying bags, through orchards
and over paths. This one, maybe. It is getting late,
though, for that sort of imagining. The sidewalks are full
of shoppers shoving to get by. The girls
ride pertly on their motorbikes. Downtown
on the Croisette, the new tourists are buying
perfumes and blankets while the single organ tone,
the pedal note of the luxury ship, calls them
with the deepest and richest sound, but one sound only,
back to supper and another port, finally
back to New York. Now from the balcony,
looking down the valley onto the ocean,
I think of Dachau, which has been so well scrubbed
and manicured it is more horrible for it.
There on the assembly ground I saw the tops
of churches in the village, and straight ahead
in a lovely grove were the gas ovens.
Now it is all a museum. Here on the south coast
I can't see anything beyond the elbows of Europe,
beyond the smoke from the *Michaelangelo*,
beyond the islands or the line where the gray sky
blurs with the water. "Out there somewhere," we say
and stop. If we were God, what would we do?

1967

Winter Poem for All My Rejections And Those I am Sending

But for this horrible cold. We are so glutted,
but never think we don't love you. Couldn't settle
strongly enough. We love you no crap.
Those marvelous lines are not what we need.
Hit us again. *Like thousands of tiny bombs.*
Try splitting your poems in half, to relieve congestion.

Sorry. These poems are sorry. At last count
they haven't won out. *I have been sending you poems,*
timing the nice lines to go off all year.
They are charming but not shocking enough.
This cold is horrible. Unfortunately it is impossible
to thank you in one of our personal letters.

On Depositing My Papers, Etc., In The Boston University Library

Here are his manuscripts, starting with a poem
on roller skates and ending with the unfinished cycle
"Love." We have every scrap, including these boxes
of letters from his mother, these pictures, tapes
of his readings, and several envelopes sealed
for seventy-five years. Here is a lock
of his baby hair, proving he was blond
at birth, falling gradually to baldness.
Here is a pudding he once left half eaten.
Here are his teeth, and in this glass cabinet
the spleen, liver and gall sac that added their parts
to the poems. In this refrigerated drawer
Is Frost himself. Beyond here the collection
naturally expands to several rooms of letters
from his friends and the letters his friends wrote
to their friends and received from their friends.
Everything that mattered to the poet is here.
In this room, under ideal archival conditions,
we have his friends, and in here his enemies and their friends
and their toothbrushes, aprons, tree houses, cameras, tableware.
Here on the wall are his friends' wives
and here in this antechamber his readers,
who persist in turning moldy. Someday, we hope,
we shall be able to reconstruct the poet,
or something reasonably close—even better, perhaps—
and probably with a good deal of material left over.

Steps

I.

Now that it's time for nothing else,
you pack the dishes, clothing, books
and furniture, square things with the bank
and all the stores, kill the lights
and telephone, fill in the pink card
at the post office, kiss the neighbors
and back the car out of the drive.
The old house stares from its holes
like a tired drunk, and you know the road
swims under your wheels to the flat lake
that is memory with its narrow source
and dark lagoons swept by no breezes.

II.

Voices, of course voices. At times
Judy is back, or sweet Harold.
Yet there is more. Stare at the wall,
a ring or a photo, and slowly comes
the feeling, what it was to be nimble
of breath and sinew, the idea of warm
early mornings one particular year—
not only the smell of flowers or grass
or whistles from a distant station,
but the whole sense of the body. It goes.
The harder you hold, the more smoothly it vanishes.
Patient you wait, grown heavy and gentle.

On Finding the Remains of A Crystal Radio

Altitude lost, cracked-up on a sheer plateau,
Jack Armstrong worried me for an episode
while elephants thundered, 500 feet below,
toward their graveyard, guarded by Pygmy arrows.
Villains named Dirk sneered and gnashed as they
 ambushed my heroes.

Transmitting from a sinister studio:
the Green Hornet with his incredible car,
and Inner Sanctum—complete with creaking door,
bloodsucking, traded brains, and a severed hand
that played while the pianist boiled in hell. Below,

while I slept wrinkles in my turning mind,
I felt the boom of my father's console set
meaninglessly tuned to another station.
Then bugs built webs and shells inside the earphones,
wires broke, my coils unwound. Today I've found

this lump of crystal like a saved tooth
to roll in the palm, to bite the memory
and sing a dreaming thread of lies and truth
it played into my head for several years
until I turned it down for poetry.

Death Entered the World

Death entered the world, Bushmen tell,
when a rabbit had a fight with the moon
about the treatment of corpses. "Bury them,"
the rabbit said. "Otherwise the smell
will be unbearable." He twitched his nose
and trembled at the thought
of corpses bloating in an August sun.

The moon explained, "You have your eyes too low
to see the answer. Listen to one who knows.
Dead creatures should be brought to life again."
"Ridiculous," the rabbit cried, and leaped
high enough to scratch the full cheeks
of the moon—the marks are there. And in its pain
the moon split the hare's lip with a knife.

Each has what it argued for. The moon
grows thin and dies, then comes again to life.
But whenever a rabbit dies, it dies.
"And people, too," the Bushmen say, "We, too,"
knowing the facts of burial, yet preferring
to remember the quaint legend that something in the sky
once offered a lofty alternative and was bitterly turned down.

The Snow Goose

Today in the frozen swamp you were correct
about the honking, son; again you were right.
No animal, I said, could make that noise
and sent you through the pines to flush some grouse

or rabbits down across the clean ice
where I could depend upon the luxury
of an open shot. A hundred yards
ahead, two squirrels ran up their hollow tree.

But nothing from the pines. Quiet and cold
over an inch of snow, around the clumps
of brittle grass, we made toward the river,
hoping to surprise the black ducks.

Then again the sound—a horn on a train
or on a building calling men to work.
I led us slowly through a wood,
knowing what was and what wasn't there.

Out of the trees, we saw it in the wide
stream like a small white feathered boat with a head
turning everywhere, and that noise it made
for more geese, yet was the only one.

The hanging, the wine, nothing can make a wild
white goose tender and not taste like fish.
Once, in good faith, a friend gave me this beautiful bird,
and we could hardly swallow its stringy flesh.

Today it honked and maneuvered, the snow goose
paddling in season by us, around the bend,
past the summer cabins, under the bridge,
beside the local airport, by the farms

and down the Susquehanna, for all I know,
to Baltimore. It could have the river.
You and I, the predators, went back
into the trees and shot a fat brown hare.

Carol, On the Floor

The blanket a shroud, you roll your neck in sleep's
discomfort as I write. Lioness,
you guard, while I must be awake,
my dreams, knowing I would tear
the knife from any who would drive your eyes
too deep to open when our vigils end.

I Love You In Syracuse Drunk and Apprehensive All During the Moon Landing

We knew we were in the country—the road signs
rusty with bullet holes, and we heard on the radio
about Martin Luther King's brother drowning in his pool
and Edward Kennedy driving into the water,
killing that blonde, and how the Highgate Cemetery
makes $960 a year, charging people to be photographed
near Marx's grave. Death is everywhere
today, except on the moon. You and I
are trying to resuscitate our love, distracted
by Houston, finally entering a restaurant
with color t.v., watching the jerky moon walks
of the astronauts. You and I are trying
hard to dock ourselves before Apollo's arrows
insert us into separate orbits, while Syracuse finds,
as everyone finds, the moon landing fantastic
while counting its 59th traffic fatality
and enjoying that poor Russian Luna 15 that was smashed
to the surface.
And from some station here is Kate Smith
advertising coffee, really great tasting instant
favorite Chase & Sanborn when the moon comes
over the mountain, and the Nixon administration
will now let me go to Communist China
because I am a teacher, but you and I
are in love, God damn, despite the Nettleton Shoe
mid-season clearances. Man has again scored
one of his awesome achievements, and most area businessmen
have conducted their normal hustle and bustle. All
the vital city services of police and fire are ready,
though workers tomorrow morning may report bleary eyed.

And a grinding two-car mishap on West Fayette Street
has killed a young marine in a car driven
by another marine. And I still love you,
while other victims are listed in good condition,
and others are about to undergo surgery
if all the blood groups would only report to the bank,
and we should get turned on by Grand Prix styling.
This city has us pegged, and we could take delivery today
of those eye-catching bell-bottomed slacks
from Casual Korner, with all the regular citizens
commenting on the Apollo moon landing.
What do you think man will do next, now
that he has landed? They hope it will make a better environment
and are reminded of Christopher Columbus, one of the greatest
   things
that ever happened, and want to be around
when they land on Mars, and didn't believe in airplanes
either. We are in Central New York,
a continuing successful flight, accessed successfully
with TCP keeping our plugs from fouling.
I love you with that good mileage gasoline
and all the soil and rock samples and the refuse
left on the moon surface. Someday may we travel
to a roped-off shrine in our command module
swimmingly, and all the positive assessments
of our love will reach to the smallest settlements
where finance offices all across the void
make our money go further, depending on
how much the friendly loaners can lend us.

All the lunar samples will be out of quarantine,
and someday we will be out of quarantine,
putting our money into the right places
with the life blood of the United States,
never giving up our drive for knowledge;
and if we think we've got problems now, think what will happen
if the average Congressman lets us fall behind
in the search for technology, and now those three are back
in their combined capsule, and we must get moving
to get together, love, before something terrible happens to us.

Poems for Carol

I.

I say the trouble with this bus ride
is that it is neither from you nor to you.
From some place to some place, however, I am watching
for myself, for the glimpses of interest
that mean I am more than either of us thought
he was without the other. Two black children
in front of me have said good-bye happily
to their bearded father. They must be on vacation.
And somewhere inside my glimpses of the waving,
their comforted eyes, I guess that I am myself,
deep, voting for myself, which is not ungenerous
when, elected, I can show you pages and faces
and send our campaign promises beyond law,
beyond travel to get to some place, beyond
the partisan kisses we have joined in,
so that even this cold tangent is a barnstorm,
a stirrup cup of our blood, so that tomorrow
whenever I savor the road we can take it.

II.

Past the Discount Centers, Left-Over Sales,
I re-train myself to grow our best rules
for each of us. Though we have broken our names,
our promises, our goals like the egg that bloomed
inside you and then tore its flowers down
into your toilet, gracefully you have run
us closer to a love we will bear
as this bus dances, fulfilled by its glad fire,
moved by hands taught to be heavy and delicate
—expressed, free, knowing how to discover and follow.